STRANGE BUT TRUE

Books by Vernon Coleman include:

The Medicine Men (1975)

Paper Doctors (1976)

Stress Control (1978)

The Home Pharmacy (1980)

Aspirin or Ambulance (1980)

Face Values (1981)

The Good Medicine Guide (1982)

Bodypower (1983)

Thomas Winsden's Cricketing Almanack (1983)

Diary of a Cricket Lover (1984)

Bodysense (1984)

Life Without Tranquillisers (1985)

The Story Of Medicine (1985, 1998)

Mindpower (1986)

Addicts and Addictions (1986)

Dr Vernon Coleman's Guide To Alternative Medicine (1988)

Stress Management Techniques (1988)

Know Yourself (1988)

The Health Scandal (1988)

The 20 Minute Health Check (1989)

Sex For Everyone (1989)

Mind Over Body (1989)

Eat Green Lose Weight (1990)

How To Overcome Toxic Stress (1990)

Why Animal Experiments Must Stop (1991)

The Drugs Myth (1992)

Complete Guide To Sex (1993)

How to Conquer Backache (1993)

How to Conquer Pain (1993)

Betrayal of Trust (1994)

Know Your Drugs (1994, 1997)

Food for Thought (1994, revised edition 2000)

The Traditional Home Doctor (1994)

People Watching (1995)

Relief from IBS (1995)

The Parent's Handbook (1995)

Men in Dresses (1996)

Power over Cancer (1996)

Crossdressing (1996)

How to Conquer Arthritis (1996)

High Blood Pressure (1996)

How To Stop Your Doctor Killing You (1996, revised edition 2003)

Fighting For Animals (1996)

Alice and Other Friends (1996)

Spiritpower (1997)

How To Publish Your Own Book (1999)

How To Relax and Overcome Stress (1999)

Animal Rights – Human Wrongs (1999)

Superbody (1999)

Complete Guide to Life (2000)

Strange But True (2000)

Daily Inspirations (2000)

Stomach Problems: Relief At Last (2001)

How To Overcome Guilt (2001)

How To Live Longer (2001)

Sex (2001)

We Love Cats (2002)

England Our England (2002)

Rogue Nation (2003)

People Push Bottles Up Peaceniks (2003)

The Cats' Own Annual (2003)

Confronting The Global Bully (2004)

Saving England (2004)

Why Everything Is Going To Get Worse Before It Gets Better (2004)
The Secret Lives of Cats (2004)
The Cat Basket (2005)

novels
The Village Cricket Tour (1990)
The Bilbury Chronicles (1992)
Bilbury Grange (1993)
Mrs Caldicot's Cabbage War (1993)
Bilbury Revels (1994)
Deadline (1994)
The Man Who Inherited a Golf Course (1995)
Bilbury Pie (1995)
Bilbury Country (1996)
Second Innings (1999)
Around the Wicket (2000)
It's Never Too Late (2001)
Paris In My Springtime (2002)
Mrs Caldicot's Knickerbocker Glory (2003)
Too Many Clubs And Not Enough Balls (2005)
Tunnel (1980, 2005)

as Edward Vernon
Practice Makes Perfect (1977)
Practise What You Preach (1978)
Getting Into Practice (1979)
Aphrodisiacs – An Owner's Manual (1983)

with Alice
Alice's Diary (1989)
Alice's Adventures (1992)

With Donna Antoinette Coleman
How To Conquer Health Problems Between Ages 50 and 120 (2003)
Health Secrets Doctors Share With Their Families (2005)

VERNON COLEMAN'S

STRANGE BUT TRUE

Illustrated by Vernon Coleman

Edited by Donna Antoinette Coleman

BLUE
BOOKS

Published by Blue Books, Publishing House, Trinity Place, Barnstaple, Devon EX32 9HG, England.

Transferred to digital print 2005

Reprinted 2006

ISBN: 1 899726 15 2

A catalogue record for this book is available from the British Library.

Printed by 4word Ltd, Bristol

Dedicated to Thomasina.

Sometimes strange but always true.

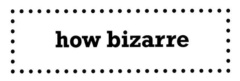

how bizarre

ACCORDING TO *The Lancet* in 1875 a bullet fired in the American Civil War on May 12 1863, carried away the left testicle of a soldier and went on to penetrate the left side of a young nurse and carry sperm into her body. Nine months later the nurse gave birth to a son. Her hymen was intact at the birth and she insisted she was still a virgin. A doctor introduced the soldier and the nurse. They later married and had three other children by conventional means.

· ·

A SAILOR who used a shipmate's plastic inflatable woman for sex caught gonorrhoea from it.

· ·

IT IS POSSIBLE for a woman to give birth to twins fathered by two different men. In 1970, in Germany, blood tests led to a court ruling that although a woman had given birth to twins, one of her babies was illegitimate.

· ·

IN 16TH CENTURY England it was customary for men to greet women in public by touching their breasts.

RESEARCHERS CHECKING litter on England's beaches found, among a mountain of other things, two intravenous drip bags and one colostomy bag.

FOUR PATIENTS – two men and two women – taking an anti-depressant drug complained that they had an orgasm every time they yawned. The men said they had to lie down and rest for ten or fifteen minutes every time they opened their mouths.

A PRESS SPOKESMAN for an American organisation was told off for wearing women's panties in his jacket breast pocket, instead of a handkerchief. He claimed that the panties went well with his tie.

• •

THERE IS A dating service in Los Angeles, California, called Hung Jury. It specialises in well-equipped men.

• •

AN AMERICAN psychiatrist says that more people should talk to themselves. It seems that having a firm word with yourself can do wonders.

• •

A GROUP OF AMERICANS urge people to take their house plants for a walk 'to make them healthier'.

IN THE 19ᵀᴴ CENTURY, Scottish surgeon Robert Liston removed a patient's leg in 33 seconds. He worked so quickly that his unfortunate assistant couldn't get his hand out of the way in time and lost three fingers.

WHEN KING CHARLES II had a fit in 1685, doctors gave him a medicine made from a human skull and put pigeon droppings on his feet.

WHEN A 91-YEAR-OLD woman died a few years ago in a nursing home, undertakers took her room-mate, who was asleep, by mistake. The error was discovered as the undertakers prepared to embalm the sleeping woman.

• •

IN THE 14TH CENTURY, headaches were thought to be caused by small demons hammering on the inside of the skull demanding to be let out. Surgeons drilled small holes in the skull in order to let the demons escape.

• •

SOUTH AMERICAN INDIANS used black ants to stitch wounds. They encouraged the ants to bite the wound together and then twisted off the ants' bodies – leaving the jaws in place as sutures.

• •

A MAN RECORDED as having died in 1978 sued the American government for social security support. The government wouldn't pay as the man had been officially certified dead. Friends said he had been brought back to life in a voodoo ceremony.

• •

AN AMERICAN PORN STAR sued two companies for using his penis as a model for mass market dildos and then failing to pay him royalties.

• •

AUSTRALIAN HEALTH OFFICIALS told a restaurant in Perth to stop using the navels of its topless waitresses as fruit dishes. A local law banning topless women from serving food already existed, but the restaurant claimed that the law didn't cover the use of belly buttons as food containers.

• •

IN THE 17TH CENTURY women who were worried about having sagging breasts were advised to put on a poultice of well-bruised green hemlock until their breasts had been restored to a good shape and consistency.

• •

THE BRAHMANS of southern India believe that a younger brother should not marry before an older one. When an older brother couldn't find a bride he was married to a tree so his younger brother would be free to marry.

• •

A YOUNG JAPANESE man who wanted to be a Sumo wrestler was, at 5ft 2 inches, six inches too small. So he had six inches of silicone implanted on top of his head.

· ·

DURING THE REIGN of Louis XIV, the Church condoned the wearing of low-necked dresses as long as women wearing them had gold rings piercing their nipples.

· ·

THE TERM HARPAZOPHILIA describes a medical condition in which individuals derive sexual pleasure from being robbed.

· ·

AN ARAB KING once boasted that although he had 400 wives he had never seen any of their faces.

⋯⋯⋯⋯⋯⋯⋯⋯⋯⋯⋯⋯⋯⋯⋯⋯⋯⋯⋯

THE BEST-SELLER LIST in Japan recently included a book called The Complete Guide to Suicide. The book described ten preferred methods, and gave each a rating of one to five skulls.

⋯⋯⋯⋯⋯⋯⋯⋯⋯⋯⋯⋯⋯⋯⋯⋯⋯⋯⋯

YOU CAN BUY a clock which tells you exactly how many hours, minutes and seconds you have left to live (based on an average life expectancy of 76 years). The clock also tells you how much time is left in your marriage (assuming that the average union lasts seven years).

⋯⋯⋯⋯⋯⋯⋯⋯⋯⋯⋯⋯⋯⋯⋯⋯⋯⋯⋯

AN AUSTRALIAN WOMAN was awarded £1 million after being shot by a lamb. She was trying to put the lamb into a truck when it kicked a rifle and sent a bullet into her waist.

⋯⋯⋯⋯⋯⋯⋯⋯⋯⋯⋯⋯⋯⋯⋯⋯⋯⋯⋯

NERVOUS INDIVIDUALS can now buy a 22lb steel plate mailbox that will survive a nuclear explosion.

• •

IN 1808 two Frenchmen, each armed with a blunderbuss, fought a duel over a woman from identically-sized balloons over the Tuileries Gardens in Paris. The man who fired first – missed. The other duellist scored a direct puncture and his rival plunged to his death.

• •

A DUTCH OPTICIAN insisted on women patients taking off their clothes and dancing while he played the accordion so he could test their suitability for contact lenses, a court heard. 'My client was trained in Britain where the practice is widespread,' said his lawyer.

• •

AFTER A COUPLE were taken to hospital locked in sexual harmony, doctors found the woman had inserted a home-made intra-uterinc device to stop herself getting pregnant. The device had wrapped itself around the man's penis, trapping it.

• •

A WELL KNOWN woman singer is reported to perform oral sex (and to swallow the result of her labours) before she goes on stage. She is said to do this 'to lubricate' her throat.

• •

ACCORDING TO the medical journal *Monitor Weekly*, doctors had to remove spectacles, a key, a tobacco pouch and a magazine from the anus of a 38-year-old man. All these items had been inserted by 'a friend'. (With friends like this, who needs an enema?)

aren't people amazing?

KITTY FISHER, history's most expensive whore, worked in the 18th Century and charged a massive 100 guineas a night. When a mean Duke gave her a mere £50 for her services she was so offended that she put the note between two slices of buttered bread and ate it for breakfast.

IN 1907, a Leicestershire man called Burnett decided he never wanted to sleep again. And so he didn't until he died in 1965.

TOP SPORTSMEN often have a resting heart rate of between 20 and 30 beats per minute. (A normal heart rate is 70.)

EDWARD KAZARIAN, a violinist in the Yerevan Symphony Orchestra, once made a statue of Charlie Chaplin which would stand inside the eye of a needle. He also painted a line of circus animals on a single human hair. Mr Kazarian used a single paintbrush and applied the paint strokes between heartbeats to keep his hand steady.

• •

SHAKESPEARE WAS responsible for the first recorded use of the word cock. He used it in 1599 in Henry IV (Part 2) to refer to an erect penis: 'And Pistol's cock is up.'

• •

QUEEN CLEOPATRA was said to have been the most famous free-love fellatrice of the ancient world. She performed oral sex on over 1,000 happy men.

• •

ARTIST SALVADOR DALI stripped a female visitor to his apartment. When she was naked he put two fried eggs on her shoulders. Then, without a word, he showed her the door.

• •

GERM-PHOBIC billionaire Howard Hughes was once trapped in a men's lavatory in Las Vegas because there were no paper towels. He wouldn't touch the handle to open the door without a towel to protect his hand from possible germs.

• •

THE TALLEST WOMAN who ever lived, Jane Bunford, was 7ft 7in. Her skeleton is in the medical school museum at Birmingham University.

• •

NORWEGIAN BORN Hans Langseth had a beard which was 17ft 6ins long when he died.

• •

CALIFORNIAN ARTIST Ronnie Nicolino used 200 volunteers to create a two-mile long sand sculpture made up of 21,000 34C sized breasts.

• •

EMPRESS WU HU of the T'ang dynasty designed a custom aimed at elevating the female and humbling the male. She insisted that all visiting dignitaries pay homage by performing oral sex on her.

• •

THE MOST FAMOUS transvestite in history was French diplomat Chevalier d'Eon de Beaumont. Born in 1728, he died aged 83 – after spending 49 years as a man and 34 as a woman.

• •

IN 1773 a man called Samuel Whitehouse, of the parish of Willenhall, sold his wife, Mary Whitehouse, to a chap called Thomas Griffiths. Mr Whitehouse received one shilling in payment. According to the contract Mr Griffiths had to accept Mrs Whitehouse with all her faults.

• •

THOMAS DIMSDALE, who inoculated Catherine the Second's family against small-pox, was made a baron and a general, plus given a fee of £10,000 and a pension of £500.

• •

MOVIE STAR Clark Gable was listed on his birth certificate as a girl.

• •

FRENCH NOVELIST Victor Hugo was such a tireless frequenter of Paris brothels that, on his death, the government gave the prostitutes 70,000 francs so that they could join the mourners in the streets without losing money.

• •

SEXUAL DISPLAY used to be seen as a sign of respect to a visitor. The Queen of Ulster and the 610 ladies of her court used to meet visitors naked from the waist up.

• •

FRENCH WRITER Honore de Balzac believed a man's sperm was linked to brain power. After losing his usual self-control in a Paris brothel, he wailed: 'I lost a novel this morning!'

• •

HERBERT 'ZEPPO' MARX got his nickname because his birth coincided with the first Zeppelin airship.

• •

LUPE VELEZ, Mexican film star of the 1940s, could rotate her left breast in both directions while the other one remained motionless.

• •

VAN GOGH didn't start drawing until he was 27.

• •

IN 1960 James W Rodgers was facing a firing squad in Utah. His final request was for a bullet-proof vest.

• •

'I'M LOOKING FOR a loophole!' said comic W.C. Fields flipping through the Bible on his death bed.

• •

KARL LUDWIG NESSLER, the German inventor of the hair perm, only became a hairdresser because his eyesight was too poor for shoe-making.

• •

VICTORIAN ACTRESS Sarah Bernhardt travelled with a silk-lined coffin. She learned her lines in it – and – entertained lovers in it too.

• •

LOUIS XIII of France married Anne of Austria when both were only 14 years old. On their wedding night they spent two hours together with nurses in attendance. Louis XIV was born seven years later.

• •

GERTRUDE STEIN bought Picasso's entire output from 1906 to 1909 because no one else wanted to buy his work. Picasso used to keep warm by burning his own drawings.

battle of the sexes

BABY GIRLS smile more than baby boys do. (Perhaps they know what the future holds).

. . . .

THE AVERAGE male brain weighs 3lb 2oz. The average female brain is 2lb 12oz.

. . . .

WOMEN ARE BETTER designed than men for survival in adverse circumstances. Their greater store of body fat means that they can stay alive longer.

. . . .

THE FASTEST MALE human swimmer can travel at 2.29 metres per second. The fastest female swimmer travels at 2 metres per second. A dolphin can swim at 11 metres per second.

. . . .

THREE TIMES more women than men draw old age pensions.

• •

MARRIED MEN live longer than single men. But single women live longer than married women.

• •

FOUR OUT OF TEN women and five out of ten men admit that if a new partner asked they would purposely underestimate the total number of their former lovers.

• •

AN AMERICAN STUDY revealed that 34 per cent of men and 10 per cent of women have lied to get a partner into bed.

• •

IF YOU ARE a woman, your red blood cells live for about 110 days. If you are a man, your red blood cells live for roughly 10 days longer.

• •

ONE IN 10 UK men and one in 20 women live alone.

• •

A SURVEY SHOWED that 21 per cent of male Danish tourists carry condoms. The same survey showed that just 6 per cent of female Danish tourists do the same.

• •

FORTY ONE PER CENT of women say they want a man with a sense of humour, but only 21 per cent of men feel a sense of humour is important in a woman; 33 per cent of men say they want a slim woman, but only 2 per cent of women feel that slenderness is important in a man; 57 per cent of men say looks are important, but only 26 per cent of women agree.

• •

ONE IN FOUR men and one in 20 women have watched a strip show or a live sex show.

• •

THE AVERAGE MAN is 5ft 8½ in tall and weighs 12st 4lb. The average woman is 5ft 3½ in and weighs 10st 6lb.

• •

COLOUR BLINDNESS affects about 8 per cent of men and 0.4 per cent of women. It usually involves a problem differentiating between red and green. If both parents are colour blind there is a 50 per cent chance all their children will be affected.

• •

MEN CAN EXPECT to live to 73. Women to 78.

• •

ACCORDING TO the World Health Organization, women suffer more mental health problems than men and are much more likely to be admitted to mental hospitals.

• •

THE AVERAGE WORKING woman spends three hours a day on housework and 50 minutes with her children. The average working man does 17 minutes housework and spends 12 minutes with his children.

• •

AT BIRTH, there are about 105 baby boys for every 100 girls. At 18, there are 100 males for every 100 females. At the age of 67 there are 70 males to every 100 females. At the age of 100 there are just 21 males to every 100 females.

• •

THE AVERAGE woman sleeps 25 minutes more each night than the average man.

• •

THE AVERAGE male orgasm lasts eight seconds. If a man has an orgasm twice a week for 40 years, he will spend nine hours in ecstasy. Because the average female orgasm lasts 20 seconds, a woman who had the same number of orgasms, spread over the same number of years, would spend 23 hours enjoying them.

• •

MORE THAN 100,000 British citizens who were born male live as women.

• •

MARRIED MEN watch 60 minutes more TV each day than their wives.

carry on doctor

FOUR THOUSAND years ago doctors in Babylon who made mistakes had their hands cut off.

· ·

DOCTORS ARE up to three times more likely to commit suicide than anyone else.

· ·

BETWEEN 10 AND 13 per cent of doctors will, at some time in their careers, become drug or alcohol abusers.

· ·

IN ANCIENT CHINA doctors were paid by patients when they were healthy – but when the patients fell sick the doctors paid them.

· ·

FOUR OUT OF FIVE soviet doctors are women.

• •

A REPORT SHOWED that doctors' stethoscopes are often contaminated with staphylococci and can spread infection from one patient to another. When 29 doctors were interviewed only three had ever cleaned their stethoscopes.

• •

FOUR OUT OF TEN doctors have been assaulted by a patient. (Though probably not all by the same patient.)

• •

AN AMERICAN SURVEY shows that one in ten doctors have had sex with at least one of their patients.

• •

A THIRD OF the patients for whom doctors prescribe drugs take them properly – and follow the instructions they have been given. One third follow their doctor's advice (more or less). And a third don't bother to take their drugs at all.

• •

HALF OF THE patients who visit British family doctors will be in and out of the surgery in less than five minutes.

'Next!'

• •

TWO THIRDS of Britain's GPs would like to quit medicine and do something else for a living. Nearly as many hospital doctors are depressed and dissatisfied with their work, according to surveys conducted by two medical magazines.

• •

TWO PATHOLOGISTS who performed more than 400 post-mortems found that in more than half the cases the doctors looking after the deceased patients had made the wrong diagnosis.

• •

BRITISH DOCTORS spend only 12 per cent of their time with their patients. (What do they do with the rest of their time? I don't know. But an awful lot of them are good at golf).

• •

FRENCH DOCTOR Charles Felix, who treated Louis XIV's painful piles, received a farm, a title and a massive cash fee.

• •

A STUDY OF 500 doctors showed that 59 per cent had used psychoactive drugs at some time in their lives.

• •

MEDICAL KNOWLEDGE is doubling every eight years. This means most doctors are out of date for most of the time they are in practice.

• •

AMERICAN DOCTORS claim that excessive smiling is bad for your health and can cause a painful joint condition. (The disease is virtually unknown among traffic wardens, undertakers and traffic policemen.)

• •

DOCTORS IN the 17th Century prepared their own medicines. Common ingredients included dried vipers, worms, foxes' lungs, powdered precious stones, ants' oil, butter made during the month of May and moss taken from the skulls of murder victims.

• •

A SURVEY OF junior hospital doctors showed that a quarter admitted giving a drug to the wrong patient and a quarter admitted giving the wrong dose.

• •

DOCTORS WHO are rude, inaccessible, poor at communicating and always in a hurry are more likely to be sued than patient, kind and sympathetic doctors.

• •

GPS HAVE SHOWN that patients who listen to music over headphones while having intimate examinations experience less anxiety.

• •

IN 1970, one in five medical students believed a woman must have an orgasm in order to conceive. Most of those students will now be respected doctors.

law and order

In 1938, the King of Bavaria issued a law forbidding civilians from growing moustaches. Police were given the power to shave offending citizens.

ACCORDING TO official guidelines in the USA the required prison sentence for possession of 1,000 dollars worth of LSD is 10 years. The prison sentence for attempted murder is 6.5 years and for rape it is 6 years. For armed robbery the required sentence is 4.7 years and for theft of at least 50 million dollars a more modest 4 years.

• •

IN IRAN the punishment for anyone successfully prosecuted three times for the production or sale of pornographic videos is death.

• •

PEEPING TOMS used to be immune to arrest if they were over 50 years of age or had only one eye.

• •

AFTER JOHN WILKES BOOTH shot USA president Abraham Lincoln, he broke his leg fleeing the scene of the assassination. He called on a local doctor called Dr Samuel Mudd for help. Dr Mudd was jailed for life for treating Wilkes although he didn't know what Wilkes had done. Mudd, who is immortalised in the phrase 'his name is mud', later got a pardon for stopping a yellow fever epidemic in the prison where he was serving his sentence.

• •

EATING A CORPSE is not illegal according to English law.

• •

IT IS ILLEGAL to make love in a puddle in Swaziland.

• •

A GERMAN WHO wanted to use the loo on an American plane was told to sit down by the stewardess. He replied: 'No, the roof will go if I sit.' This is a literal translation of German slang meaning 'I'm desperate to go.' But the attendant assumed it meant he had a bomb. The plane immediately landed and the man was thrown in jail. He was freed nine months later by a judge who could speak German.

• •

LAWS AGAINST sodomy have been traced to the Emperor Justinian (483-562 AD) who believed the act caused earthquakes.

• •

IT IS LEGAL to make love in a car in New Jersey as long as you don't sound the horn.

• •

AN AMERICAN MOTHER lost custody of her 12-year-old son and received a 45-day jail sentence and a $200 fine after hiring a stripper for her son's birthday party and allowing him to lick whipped cream off the girl's chest.

• •

A CATHOLIC PRIEST was arrested in Florida charged with shoplifting a pack of condoms.

• •

POLICE WHO SUSPECT that couples in the town of Coeur d'Alenc, Idaho, are having sex in a parked car must pull up behind the vehicle, honk three times and wait two minutes before knocking on the door or window.

• •

A COMPUTER PROGRAMME designed to offer legal advice is being taken to court in Texas – because it is considered a possible threat to lawyers.

• •

MAKING LOVE in a car is legal in Detroit, Michigan – but only if you are parked on your own driveway.

• •

IT IS ILLEGAL to carry an ice cream cone in your pocket in Lexington Kentucky.

• •

A JUDGE in Texas sentenced a 31-year-old man to 35 years in jail for stealing a 12oz can of Spam.

• •

ERROL FLYNN was jailed three times for assault – the last time for hitting a policeman.

• •

A court in Illinois fined a fetishist 500 dollars after he tricked 50 women into giving him their underwear.

• •

It is illegal for a woman to show her toes in public in Laos.

oh boy!

EJACULATED SPERM leaves the human penis faster than a sprinter leaves the blocks.

. . . .

THE LARGEST PENIS ever measured was 13 inches long.

. . . .

THE AVERAGE QUANTITY of sperm produced in a single ejaculation is 5mls – a teaspoonful. The world record is 31cc – two soup spoonfuls.

. . . .

ONE IN THREE men has had a condom break during sex and hasn't told his partner.

. . . .

NINE OUT OF 10 men lose their virginity before their 19th birthday.

• •

DURING HIS LIFETIME the average male spends the equivalent of 10 working weeks shaving.

• •

A SURVEY HAS shown that men consider a nice bottom just as important as intelligence when trying to find an ideal woman.

• •

MORE THAN HALF of British men say they regard at least one of the women with whom they work as being sexually attractive.

• •

UP TO ONE in seven cases of chronic impotence are caused by penile injuries sustained during masturbation or intercourse.

• •

THE AVERAGE man has 30,000 whiskers on his face.

• •

JUST OVER 1 in 100 married men have had at least one male sexual partner in the last five years.

• •

A MAN PRODUCES 72 million sperm a day – enough to populate the entire world in three months.

• •

THE DISTANCE a man fires his semen varies. The world record is 8ft 8ins. The ancient Hebrews used to believe that sperm which didn't come out forcefully wasn't fertile.

• •

ONE MAN in 50 has sex at least once a day.

• •

MOST MEN believe that job satisfaction and a good car are more important than a hot sex life.

• •

MEN HAVE grown breasts after eating meat from a chicken which has been injected with female hormones to encourage growth.

• •

ONE IN 14 boys is circumcised by the age of 15. But less than a quarter of circumcisions are medically necessary. Many circumcisions are done for religious reasons or simply because someone, usually the boy's mother, thinks that a circumcised penis looks nicer. Like all operations, circumcision can occasionally be fatal. Surveys suggest that men who are circumcised have less satisfactory sex lives than men who are not.

• •

MORE THAN a quarter of American men aged 30 to 34 are not married. Twenty years ago the figure was less than 10 per cent.

• •

TWO MILLION British men are impotent.

• •

MEN WHO EAT a high fat diet are nearly twice as likely to develop prostate cancer as those on low-fat diets.

• •

MORE THAN FIVE out of 10 men complain that their partners are invariably too tired to make love.

• •

AVERAGE SPERM COUNTS have halved in the last 50 years. No-one knows why. Possible causes include the presence of female hormones in drinking water. The hormones get in the water because women who have taken the contraceptive pill pass the hormones out in their urine and the water purifying systems don't remove them.

• •

SIX OUT OF TEN men say they wish their partner would make the first move in bed more often and one in six men say they would prefer their female partners to spend more time on foreplay.

• •

ONE THIRD OF all men admit that they never do any exercise at all.

• •

IN VICTORIAN ENGLAND men zealously avoided ejaculating whenever they could in the belief that an ejaculate's ingredients came in limited quantities and that wanton waste could be potentially fatal.

• •

ACCORDING TO a 7th Century writer a man who copulated with 93 women would attain immortality.

• •

A HUGE MAJORITY of men disapprove of homosexual activities. Most men would prefer it if sex between men was made illegal again.

• •

MEN WITH DEEP voices have more testosterone in their bodies and are likely to be more highly-sexed than men with high-pitched voices.

• •

THE AVERAGE MAN has 100 orgasms a year at the age of 20. This falls to 94 a year at 30 and 84 a year at 40.

• •

MEN ARE MORE LIKELY to look at a woman's legs than they are to look at her breasts.

• •

ONE IN FIVE men in Birmingham use prostitutes.

• •

THE AVERAGE PENIS gets bigger as its owner gets older.

• •

DURING THE 18th Century a group of men used to go out every night to stand women on their heads and look at their petticoats.

this and that

AN AMERICAN football player was accused of sexual assault by a girl student who happily made love with him at a post-game party, but got upset when she discovered that he was a member of the team she didn't support.

ATTRACTIVE MEN and women earn, on average, five per cent more than people with average looks – who, in turn, earn five to ten per cent more than plain or ugly people.

WORLD HEALTH ORGANIZATION guidelines suggest that more than a third of British penises exceed the British Standard Institute's standard dimensions for condoms and are, therefore, more likely to split or come off. In contrast studies show that most German penises are too small for European standard condoms.

ONE IN FIVE British mothers under the age of 24 are single – twice as many as in the rest of Europe.

• •

MALARIA-CARRYING mosquitoes can survive lengthy flights trapped inside luggage in the hold.

• •

THE WORLD balancing-on-one-foot record is held by a man who stood on one foot for 34 hours without falling over or holding on to anything.

• •

DIRTY DISH CLOTHS are a common source of infection in kitchens.

• •

TRAVELLING BY scheduled aircraft is four times as safe as travelling by bus, thirty times as safe as travelling by car and sixty times as safe as travelling by small plane.

• •

YOUR CHANCE of being killed by bits falling off an aeroplane is one in 10 million.

• •

YOUR CHANCE of being eaten by a shark is 1 in 300 million.

• •

THE AVERAGE BRITON drinks around 200 pints of beer and 15 bottles of wine a year.

• •

THE RECORD FOR surviving without food or water is held by an 18 year old youth who was accidentally locked in a cell by Austrian police – and then forgotten for 18 days.

• •

A QUARTER OF a million bacteria occupy a space no larger than the full stop at the end of this sentence.

• •

A POLL OF 1,000 people showed that while less than a third fear death, nearly half say they are frightened of public speaking.

• •

A GOOD RUNNER can reach about 25 m.p.h. when racing flat out.

• •

THE RISK OF BEING seriously injured in a car accident increases by more than 50 per cent on Fridays when the date is the 13th.

• •

AMERICANS THROW away 10 million computers every year.

• •

IT'S A MYTH THAT CD players give better sound reproduction. German researchers have found that only 1 in 40 music buffs can distinguish between the sound made by CDs and old fashioned LPs.

• •

ASKING FOR a date can be dangerous in politically correct America. At one American college unwelcome invitations can be punished.

• •

THE FORMER Soviet Union produces 25 times more hashish than the rest of the world put together – cannabis crops grow on 7.5 million acres.

• •

OPIUM POPPIES have been planted on 1,000 square kilometres of radioactive land around Chernobyl.

• •

NINE OUT OF ten wives and husbands who suspect their partners of being unfaithful are correct.

• •

THE WORLD'S FIRST cannabis museum, officially the Hash Information Museum, is now open in Amsterdam.

• •

THE GERMANS regard red fingernails as a sign of laziness, boredom and lack of self-confidence but red nail varnish was first used by Chinese soldiers who wanted to frighten their enemies by making it look as though their hands were dripping blood.

• •

MORE THAN a quarter of USA medical schools have eliminated animal laboratories. (And if they could do so why couldn't the others?)

• •

ROMAN SOLDIERS were partly paid in salt. Hence the phrase 'He isn't worth his salt'.

• •

THE MOST FAMOUS Biblical instance of incest was Abraham, who married his half-sister, the daughter of his father but not his mother.

• •

A FORMER AFRICAN chief had a party trick. When mounting his horse, he would leap into the saddle, sword in hand, and simultaneously decapitate the slave who was holding his stirrup. (And you thought your boss was bad.)

• •

JOSHUA WARD, who dealt with Charles II's dislocated thumb, was given a coach and horses and the exclusive right to drive them through St James's Park.

• •

PRISON STAFF who gave young offenders a glass of orange juice every day noticed a 47 per cent fall in anti-social behaviour.

• •

A STUDY HAS shown that 11 per cent of statements made to doctors by drug company representatives falsely describe the benefits of their companies' products.

• •

AN ACTRESS WHOSE name you'd instantly recognise has had so many face-lifts she can't close her eyes and has to sleep with them open.

• •

JAPANESE MOTHERS who want their sons to do well at school have sex with them so that they won't chase girls and neglect their studies.

• •

MARTIN VAN BUREN, 8th President of the United States, was a cross-dresser. He liked wearing his wife's lingerie.

• •

AN 80-YEAR-OLD man was arrested for shooting a 78-year-old neighbour during an argument over a broken fence between their two gardens.

• •

A QUARTER OF the people who pray every day admit they do it in the hope of receiving some material rewards. And one in 20 pray for something bad to happen to someone else.

it's a sad, sad, sad, sad world

TELEVISION FANS see 145 violent scenes in an average hour's viewing. The incidence of violence on television is increasing dramatically.

AT THE AGE OF 44, Friedrich Nietzsche, the German philosopher, put his arms around a badly-treated cab horse in the street and burst into tears. He was put in a lunatic asylum for the last 11 years of his life.

IN THE LAST 50 years planners have destroyed 97 per cent of wild flower meadows, half our ancient woods, 75 per cent of heaths and 190,000 miles of hedgerow. In return we have a lot of motorways and some supermarket car parks.

~ STRANGE BUT TRUE ~

AN AMERICAN COURT sent a voluntary worker to prison for giving a bagel to a homeless woman. Official USA policy seems to be that giving food to vagrants encourages them to continue hanging around, making everywhere look untidy.

• •

AT THE END of the 20th century only 26 per cent of recorded UK crimes were solved by the police. In 1979 the success rate was 42 per cent.

• •

THE WATER YOU GET out of your tap is, according to the standards of the European Community, probably unfit for human consumption.

• •

FEMALE STUDENTS in Turkey were, until recently, given virginity tests. Those who failed the test were expelled.

• •

A COURT DISMISSED the charge against a father being prosecuted for spanking his 10-year-old son when the father agreed to let a policeman spank him three times.

• •

BY THE TIME they qualify, nearly half of all medical students need psychotherapy.

• •

AN IMPOTENT child molester in America has been given a penile implant at taxpayers' expense.

• •

SCIENTIFIC RESEARCHERS who received grants totalling £1.25 million, shot 700 cats in the head – and concluded that a brain-injured organism will stop breathing. (Don't give money for research unless you know exactly what they're going to do with your money.)

• •

OVER 300,000 Columbian peasant families make their living growing illegal drugs. The same number make their living growing coffee.

• •

AN ESTIMATED 80 million girls and women in Africa have been circumcised – having their clitorises cut off so that they won't enjoy sex. In Egypt between 50 and 80 per cent of girls are mutilated in this way. (The circumcision of men, common in the West, is just about as pointless and barbaric.)

• •

WHEN BEIRUT HOSTAGE Terry Anderson asked the USA Government for documents relating to his kidnapping he was told that he had to provide authorisation from his captors waiving their right to privacy.

• •

~ STRANGE BUT TRUE ~

CHARLES KNOWLTON, born in 1800 in Massachusetts, was the first man to go to jail for advocating birth control. He was sentenced to three months' hard labour.

• •

SIXTY PER CENT of filed material is never looked at again.

• •

BATTERY HENS live in cages giving them less space than a sheet of A4 paper to stand on.

• •

FOUR PEOPLE have been executed in China for selling fake tax receipts.

• •

MOTHERS ABUSE their children nearly twice as often as fathers.

• •

ONE TENTH of all hospital records are lost.

• •

IN NORWAY two men used pliers to pull six gold teeth from the mouth of a motorist who was lying unconscious in his wrecked car.

• •

MORE THAN 60 per cent of federal prisoners in USA jails are drug offenders.

• •

IN NEW YORK CITY 45 per cent of all deaths at work are a result of murder.

• •

MALE AMERICAN doctors and nurses who responded to a questionnaire about attitudes to AIDS all said they wouldn't resuscitate a woman they'd just met in a bar if she had a heart attack... but admitted that they would consider sleeping with a stranger.

• •

BETWEEN 50 PER CENT and 80 per cent of operating theatre deaths blamed on anaesthetists are preventable – and are a result of incompetence or carelessness.

• •

HOSPITALS IN CHINA routinely fine single women who are found to have broken hymens. Women who are deemed to be non-virgins are ordered to write a 'self-criticism'.

• •

SOME SOUTH AFRICANS regard rat meat as a gastronomic treat – the rats they eat weigh up to 20 lbs.

animal magic

A GORILLA WEIGHS two or three times as much as the average man, but the average length of a male gorilla's penis is just one inch. In contrast the penis of a bull elephant can be 6ft long and that of the blue whale up to 10ft in length.

TWO HUNTERS TIED a stick of gelignite to a rabbit for a 'laugh'. They then lit the fuse and released the rabbit. They stopped laughing when the rabbit doubled back and hopped under their car.

CHIMPANZEES GET sex over in seven seconds. The elephant takes only thirty seconds. Americans make it last four minutes. A ferret can usually manage eight hours of sex and the average sex session between marsupial mice lasts 12 hours.

MALE APES and monkeys have a bone in their penis.

• •

MOST DOG BITE victims are bitten either by their own dogs or by those they have regular contact with. And the bite most commonly occurs in the dog's own home. Male dogs bite more than female dogs. The types of dogs, that bite most, are Staffordshire bull terriers, Jack Russell terriers and Alsatians.

• •

A BULL'S EJACULATE contains seven billion sperm.

• •

POLICE SNIFFER DOGS find it difficult to separate the trails of identical twins, compared to those of people unrelated to each other. (If we didn't douse ourselves with perfume we would all probably be able to identify one another by smell).

• •

A CAT FELL 46 storeys and survived.

• •

GORILLAS, SWANS and penguins all mate for life.

• •

THE DESERT RAT has sex up to 122 times an hour. (Except when Mrs Desert Rat complains of a headache.)

• •

A COMPLETE SEX reversal can occur in some species of domestic fowl if the left ovary is destroyed by disease. The right ovary will then develop into a functional testis. There are instances recorded where a hen started off laying eggs and finished up a cock – able to fertilise females.

. . . .

PETS HAVE TO CARRY lights on their tails at night in Ohio.

. . . .

PROSTITUTION CAN BE detected in some animals. If a baboon offers herself sexually to a male she may contrive to steal his food and he may let her keep the food in exchange for sex.

. . . .

LESBIAN RELATIONSHIPS have been observed in antelopes, horses, hamsters, mice, rats, guinea pigs and lions.

. . . .

HEDGEHOGS NEED fleas to stay alive. Remove the fleas and the hedgehog will die.

• •

LAPDOGS ORIGINALLY became popular because they attracted fleas away from their owners.

biology lesson

IT TAKES YOUR HEART 23 seconds to pump one blood corpuscle all the way round your body.

• •

YOUR BODY CONTAINS 650 muscles and 206 bones.

• •

IF THEY WERE LAID end-to-end, the blood vessels in your body would go twice round the world. That's 50,000 miles.

• •

IF YOU NEVER CUT your fingernails, they would be 6ft long by the time you reached pensionable age.

• •

YOUR SMALL INTESTINE measures about four times your height.

• •

IF ALL YOUR SKIN were peeled off, it would weigh around 6 lbs. And there would be enough skin to make two pillowslips.

• •

YOUR HEEL contains 70,000 nerve endings.

• •

THE SKIN on the palms of your hands and soles of your feet is one-20th of an inch thick. The skin on your face is ten times thinner.

• •

THE AVERAGE BRAIN contains 100,000 million cells.

• •

MESSAGES IN the brain travel at up to 250 miles an hour.

• •

IT IS THE IRIS which gives an eye its colour. A dark-coloured iris provides more protection against bright sunlight. If you have dark skin, you'll probably have dark eyes. Some people have eyes of different colours – Alexander the Great was one and pop star David Bowie is another.

• •

~ STRANGE BUT TRUE ~

THE AORTA, the largest of the human arteries, is about the same thickness as a standard garden hose.

• •

YOUR EYEBALL is a sphere nearly an inch in diameter.

• •

HUMAN EARS can distinguish 400,000 different sounds.

• •

THE SMALLEST BONES in your body are found in your ear.

• •

YOUR HEART pumps 1,800 gallons of blood around your body every day.

• •

WE LOSE, on average, between 50 and 100 hairs a day. Hairs grow for three to five years before falling out.

• •

THE SMALLEST human male penises can be under 1 cm when fully erect.

• •

THE SCIATIC NERVES, the largest nerves in your body, are as thick as a pencil.

born in the USA

A MAN IN Virginia, USA, who was convicted of shooting his mother-in-law, claimed he mistook her for a large racoon.

• •

AN AMERICAN drunk driver accidentally shot himself dead. His widow sued the gun manufacturers for $4 million on the grounds that the gun did not have safety devices for drunk drivers.

• •

A ROMAN CATHOLIC Church in Las Vegas happily accepts casino chips on its collection plates and in its gift shop. A Franciscan friar responsible for cashing them in has been nicknamed the Chip Monk.

• •

EVERY YEAR 8,000 Americans are injured by toothpicks.

• •

A 71 YEAR OLD American woman filed for divorce to end her 59 year marriage claiming that there are irreconcilable differences between her and her husband.

• •

IF YOU LIVE in California and earn more than $50,000 a year there is a one-in-four chance that you will be sued by someone (and their lawyer) wanting to relieve you of your wealth.

• •

TWO THIRDS of all the world's lawyers are American.

• •

AROUND 15,000 people in the United States are injured by vacuum cleaners every year.

• •

TWO AMERICAN authors have published a book called *How To Wash Your Face.*

. . . .

POPULAR MAGAZINE titles in America include *The Fish Sniffer, Balls and Burlaps, Muffler Digest* and *The Septic Tank News.*

. . . .

THREE MILLION Americans are homeless.

. . . .

A MARRIAGE GUIDANCE session in California broke down when the couple started to shoot at one another.

. . . .

A MAN IN South Carolina put a note demanding money into an automatic cash machine. When the machine did not respond he shot it and drove off.

. . . .

A FIRE STATION IN Washington, USA, burned for an hour before police woke up the firemen and got them to save their own building.

•••

AN AMERICAN entrepreneur has introduced a condom delivery service for spur-of-the-moment lovers who get caught short.

•••

AN 80-YEAR-OLD American who beat his wife to death told police he had heart trouble, was afraid he'd die and didn't want to leave his wife a widow.

•••

AN AMERICAN MAN, upset because of a row with his girlfriend, cut a hole in his waterbed, stuck his head through the hole – and drowned himself.

•••

AT A FUNERAL SERVICE in the United States, the minister described the deceased as a 'very disagreeable man, with little good in him, who would not be missed'.

food – glorious food!

THE AVERAGE INDIVIDUAL eats 30 tons of food in a lifetime.

. . . .

AN AVERAGE Christmas Day dinner consists of around 1,600 calories. To burn all that lot off, you would need to jog for three hours or to make love for eight hours.

. . . .

MORE THAN 1-in-10 people in the UK now follow a mainly vegetarian diet.

. . . .

JAPANESE SCIENTISTS have perfected a method of making a new type of beef-style burger from raw sewage.

. . . .

ONE KIWI FRUIT contains enough vitamin C to supply an adult for a day.

• •

WHO SAID SALADS were always healthy? A generous serving of vinaigrette dressing contains as much fat as four chocolate biscuits.

• •

CARROTS CONTAIN chemicals which mimic the effects of oestrogen and therefore act like birth control pills. Women trying to conceive should, therefore, not eat too many carrots.

• •

CHOCOLATE WAS originally introduced into Europe as an aphrodisiac.

• •

IN THE LAST 25 years the consumption of chips in Britain has doubled.

• •

SALES OF ORGANIC foods have risen nearly fourfold since 1988.

• •

THERE IS ENOUGH food in the world to feed every man, woman and child. Yet every day 40,000 children die of starvation.

• •

IT TAKES 10LB of grain to produce 1lb of beef. If we didn't feed the world's scarce resources to specially-bred animals to fatten them up we could easily eradicate hunger and starvation in developing countries.

• •

IN AN AVERAGE lifetime the average meat eater will consume 36 pigs, 36 sheep and 750 chickens and turkeys.

• •

THE AVERAGE adult eats 13lb of carrots and 222 eggs every year.

going up in smoke

A MODERATE SMOKER will burn his way through £50,000 worth of cigarettes in a lifetime of smoking.

• •

THE AMERICANS SMOKE 500 billion cigarettes a year. Western Europeans get through 600 billion. But the tobacco industry's latest success story is eastern Europe − where 700 billion cigarettes are smoked every year. (Tobacco has now killed more people than Hitler.)

• •

THE GOVERNMENT has spent far more on AIDS education than on trying to stop people smoking. But cigarettes have killed a million more Britons than AIDS since the disease was first diagnosed.

• •

SMOKERS ARE more likely to suffer back pain. American research has shown that cigarette smokers are more likely to have vertebral disc disease.

• •

BY THE AGE of ten, 40 per cent of boys and 28 per cent of girls have tried a cigarette.

• •

THE GOVERNMENT spends £35 trying to prevent each tobacco related premature death with anti-smoking advertisements and so on – and £2 million a time on anti-drug abuse propaganda.

• •

A PETROL STATION worker used an oxy-acetylene torch to remove a No Smoking sign – and the garage burst into flames.

• •

AS PEOPLE IN the West try to give up cigarettes, skilful advertising ensures that the consumption of tobacco in the third world is increasing rapidly.

you gain some, you lose some

WHEN SUCCESSFUL slimmers were surveyed around 90 per cent said they would rather be blind or have a leg amputated than be fat again.

YOU BURN UP 200 calories, on average when making love. If you have sex with someone every night for a year you will lose 21 lbs each.

CONSTANT UNSUCCESSFUL dieting – with a resultant fluctuation in body weight – increases the risk of illness and death.

ONE IN THREE adults are trying to lose weight today.

EATING USES UP 90 calories an hour. So if you're eating naked lettuce (at no more than two calories a leaf) you're probably using up more calories than you're consuming.

• •

PEOPLE WHO DON'T eat breakfast have more difficulty losing weight than people who do. Breakfast helps to kick-start the body's metabolism – the calorie-burning mechanism.

• •

MODERATE, REGULAR exercise such as walking will help your body burn up fat more effectively than vigorous exercise such as running.

• •

CRASH DIETING can affect your brain, temporarily damaging your memory and making you inattentive.

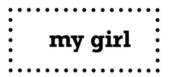

my girl

SIX-OUT-OF-TEN women own a leotard. But less than half of these women ever do any exercise.

. . . .

A STUDY IN AMERICA showed that women have a greater chance of equal employment and education in parts of the country where there is a higher circulation of pornography.

. . . .

A QUARTER OF ALL British psychiatrists are women.

. . . .

HALF OF ALL working women admit they have cried at work.

. . . .

A WOMAN'S BREASTS expand by up to one quarter when she is sexually aroused.

• •

ONE IN THREE women have made love in the kitchen.

• •

FOUR OUT OF ten women say they cry at least once a week.

• •

THE AVERAGE AGE at which married women have their first child is 27.5 years.

• •

ONE IN 12 women have been to bed with two men at once.

• •

TWO OUT OF THREE happily married women enjoy flirting – though they have no intention of being unfaithful to their partners.

• •

LESS THAN HALF the women who have affairs really enjoy them. They say they are too consumed by feelings of guilt.

• •

EIGHT OUT OF TEN women say that if a colleague they fancied wanted to have sex in office hours they would agree.

• •

THE AVERAGE BRITISH woman buys two bras and four pairs of knickers a year.

• •

NINE OUT OF TEN women have stopped menstruating by the age of 54 and virtually all have stopped by the age of 58.

• •

NEARLY HALF of all women admit that their sex lives are unsatisfactory.

• •

A THIRD OF ALL women admit they've been caught (literally) with their pants down while having sex at work.

• •

ONE IN FIVE women under the age of 40 have had some sexual contact with another woman.

• •

SIX OUT OF 10 single women are prepared to have one night stands without expecting them to lead to long-term relationships.

• •

TWO THIRDS OF married women say that they would marry their husbands again. (But one third say they wouldn't.)

• •

AMERICAN WOMEN who have breast implants may be able to claim tax relief if the operation is done to improve employment prospects.

• •

WOMEN NOW represent the fastest growing group of consumers of erotic material.

• •

BACK IN 1970 just five per cent of women had had sex by the age of 15. Today's figure is 33 per cent.

• •

WOMEN WHO drink more than two cups of coffee a day may become infertile.

• •

ONE IN THREE women regularly scream and shout during sex.

• •

A SURVEY OF 1,000 women showed that 74 per cent discuss their sex lives with their friends – and over half of these complain about their partners' performance to their friends.

• •

IN THE DAYS OF James I it was customary for young, unmarried women to walk around displaying their breasts.

• •

PUBIC HAIR CAN sometimes grow quite long. One doctor reported examining a woman who had pubic hair which stretched down as far as her knees. Another woman had her pubic hair plaited behind her back.

• •

PERFORMERS IN Parisian clubs use their vaginas to pick up and 'swallow' ping pong balls. They then fire them at the customers.

• •

WOMEN REACH orgasm more easily if their sexual partner is good-looking.

• •

ONE IN FOUR British women say they would strip in public if they were paid for it. One in five would have sex with a stranger for money. And, if given money, one in eight would appear in a porn movie and, presumably, do whatever the script required.

• •

ONE OR TWO WOMEN out of every 100 will get pregnant within a year if they rely on intra-uterine contraceptive devices.

• •

ONE IN SIX women say they would like to make love every day.

• •

THE AVERAGE psychotherapy patient is a well-educated, divorced, white woman aged in her late 30s or early 40s.

• •

ONE IN FIVE women in London have posed for nude photographs.

• •

THE AVERAGE FASHION model is 20 per cent lighter than the average woman of her height. Most models weigh less than nine out of 10 women.

• •

ONE IN TWENTY women have done the housework completely naked. One in four women say they have done the housework dressed only in their undies.

money, money, money

A HIP REPLACEMENT operation costs between £5,000 and £7,000.

AMERICA SPENDS far more on health than any other country. But America ranks near the bottom of the world's 'developed' nations when health care quality is measured.

PILFERING BY STAFF costs the British National Health Service over £180 million a year.

GOVERNMENT SPENDING now swallows up half the national income in 75 countries.

A NEW YORK secretary was awarded nearly $5 million for being sexually harassed by her boss.

• •

AN AMERICAN woman who bought coffee in a fast food restaurant and spilt the coffee on herself was awarded $2 million in damages.

• •

LOVERS IN THE USA buy 550 million condoms (worth £200 million) each year.

• •

AN AMERICAN jury awarded nearly £130,000 compensation to a woman whose fiancé changed his mind about marrying her. She had proposed and they had been together just two months.

• •

A NEW YORKER who had eye surgery revealed that the bill from the anaesthetist who put drops in his eye and stood by for 15 minutes was $547.50 (about £365).

• •

HENRY CLELAND, who wrote the novel Fanny Hill, sold his book in 1749 for 20 guineas to a bookseller who made £10,000 from it.

• •

THE WORLD'S HIGHEST-PAID investment adviser is Chevalier Harry D Schultz, who charges £1,600 an hour (£2,300 at weekends).

• •

SOCIAL SECURITY PAYMENTS, now running at £90,000 million a year, exceed Britain's entire revenue from Income Tax.

• •

AN AMERICAN collector paid £300 for an unopened packet of 1962 cornflakes.

• •

A WOMAN IN California sued the Roman Catholic Church for £13 million claiming that an unknown priest was the father of her child. She claimed to have had sex with seven priests.

anyone for sex

A SURVEY SHOWED that most people would rather have quite nice sex in a clean house than sensational, mind-blowing, groin-tingling, heart-stopping sex in a dirty house.

SEX BETWEEN consenting but unmarried adult heterosexuals is illegal in nine American states. Oral sex – both giving and receiving – is illegal in 20 American states.

COLD BATHS boost the production of sex hormones.

THE AVERAGE love-making session lasts ten minutes from first caress to final groan.

THE MOST POPULAR sexual position is the missionary position – generally favoured by 60 per cent of adults. The same proportion prefer to have sex with the lights off.

• •

TURKISH SULTANS had as many as 1,200 concubines to satisfy their every sexual whim. But they weren't as happy as you might expect. One sultan, Mustafa III, had affairs with women outside his harem. Another, Osman III, didn't like women at all and used to wear shoes with nails in the soles – so that women hired to ply him with sexual favours would hear him coming and get out of his way.

• •

EACH DAY around the world 910,000 women get pregnant and 350,000 men and women contract a sexually transmitted disease. (If that depresses you, remember that 99 million just have a good time having sex).

• •

THERE IS A chemical in semen which opens the cervix, making it easier for sperm to swim up into the womb and for a woman to give birth. Because of this it is common in some countries for pregnant women to have sex to bring on labour.

• •

IF RICE CROPS are in danger of falling, villagers in Java are expected to have sex as often as they can to help ensure the fertility of the crops.

• •

DURING SEX THE average lover's heart rate rises from around 69 beats a minute to about 115 at orgasm. It falls back to 69 within two minutes. This is roughly what you would expect from climbing two flights of stairs.

• •

IN OLD JEWISH law the punishment for anyone caught masturbating was execution.

• •

WHEN THE FRENCH government tried to stop a sexually explicit radio talk show which was broadcast every night on radio in France (and gave the station 48 hours to stop broadcasting lewd remarks) 375,000 listeners phoned in to protest, 40,000 signed a petition and 10,000 supporters gathered outside the radio station's headquarters. The government quickly backed down.

• •

A NEW LAW has been introduced in Wyoming, USA, making it illegal to have sex while standing inside a walk-in refrigerator. (Sex is presumably still legal inside walk-in refrigerators if you do it lying down.)

• •

A SURVEY OF people who put personal advertisements in magazines showed that 73 per cent were looking purely for sex.

• •

TEENAGE PUPILS in the United States who have already had sex have been told that they can consider themselves 'secondary virgins' if they stop doing it.

• •

ONE IN 10 TEENAGE couples have sex on a first date if neither drink alcohol. If both drink alcohol, one in five have sex on their first date.

• •

THE PENALTY FOR having sex with a live cod is life in prison. But you can have sex with a dead cod from a fishmonger with no worries.

• •

THE MORE SEX hormone there is circulating in your blood – and the greater your sex drive – the less your chances of being a professional or business success. Criminals and the unemployed have the highest levels of sex hormone – along with sports stars and actors.

• •

HAVING SEX – or even thinking about it – makes a man's hair grow faster.

• •

MEN AND WOMEN who enjoy good sex lives are less likely to suffer from heart disease.

• •

A NEWSLETTER IS available called Celebrate the Self: The Newsletter for the Solo Sex Enthusiast.

• •

REGULAR SEX can help prevent gout by reducing serum uric acid levels.

• •

THE JAPANESE spend as much on buying sex as their government spends on education.

• •

A SURVEY IN California showed that most couples who rekindle an old romance claim that sex is better the second time around.

• •

SPERM CAN LIVE for two days inside a woman's body after sex.

• •

PROSTITUTES DANCED naked at the court of Pope Alexander VI. Prizes were then given to the men who had sex with the most women.

did you know?

QUEEN CHRISTINE of Sweden had a tiny cannon built so she could fire tiny cannonballs at the fleas in her bedroom.

. . . .

ELVIS PRESLEY used to have a motorised exercise bicycle.

. . . .

CHEMISTS RECOMMENDED eating powdered diamonds to treat different illnesses in the 13th Century. Several famous people died from diamond overdose, including Frederick II of Germany and Pope Clement.

. . . .

CLEOPATRA WAS first married to her brother, who was also her uncle. She had him murdered at the age of 12. As you do.

. . . .

IN THE 18ᵀᴴ CENTURY the London Stock Exchange maintained its own brothel.

• •

THE DEAD SEA is 1,300ft below sea level and is the lowest point on the Earth's surface. The water contains 32 per cent salt. (Ordinary sea water contains four per cent).

• •

BY FLYING IN A V formation, birds nearly double the distance they can fly. Birds take it in turns to fly in front because the air resistance is lower for the birds at the back.

• •

IN THE AVERAGE household someone spends 500 hours a year washing up.

• •

SKETCHES BY Leonardo Da Vinci (1452-1519) show that he invented early versions of the tank, spectacles, aeroplane, alarm clock, telescope, life-jacket, air conditioning, machine gun, motor car and parachute.

• •

A BROTHEL WAS established by contemporaries of George III in houses near London's St James's Palace. Only the king's most intimate friends were allowed to frequent the brothel.

• •

TABLE TENNIS was invented by Army officers in 1810. They used a row of books for a net, cigar-box lids as bats and a champagne cork as a ball.

• •

SOCRATES, Pythagoras, Plato, Ovid, Tolstoy, Milton, Shelley and Isaac Newton were all vegetarians.

• •

FOUR OUT OF 10 computer users have at some time felt like throwing their machines out of the window.

• •

IN 1900 a lower middle class household was considered to be one employing fewer than three servants.

• •

A GERMAN court has ruled that cannabis is medically safer than alcohol or tobacco.

· ·

ALEXANDRA THE GREAT once had an entire village demolished and thrown into a river to make a bridge.

· ·

YOUNG CHILDREN laugh an average of 450 times a day. Adults laugh an average of 15 times a day.

· ·

JAPANESE SAMURAI warriors are trained to pull their testicles up inside their bodies when they fight.

· ·

IF ALL THE LIVING creatures on earth were weighed, ants would account for 10 to 15 per cent of the total weight.

· ·

BY THE AGE OF 65 you will have spent between 5,000 and 10,000 hours in the loo – that's about one year of your life.

· ·

BEFORE THE 15TH Century no self-respecting Englishwoman would consider a career in acting. So all casting for plays was done in brothels.

· ·

THE BLACK DEATH arrived in Britain after rich Genoese merchants took shelter in the city of Cafa to escape an attacking band of Tartars. When the Tartars got fed up of waiting they started to throw plague-ridden corpses over the city with catapults. At the end of the two-year siege the merchants went home, taking the plague to Northern Europe for the first time.

• •

IF YOU LIVE TO 65, you are likely to have spent 12 years of your life watching television.

• •

THE AVERAGE INDIVIDUAL speaks for no more than ten minutes a day.

• •

WHEN RONALD REAGAN was a film star he is said to have paid his mum 75 dollars a week to sign his autographs.

• •

DURING THE BOER WAR the Boers offered £25 for the capture – dead or alive – of a journalist called Winston Churchill.

• •

AT LEAST 60 churches claim to have supplies of the Virgin Mary's breast milk. She was obviously a good provider.

• •

EVERY DAY 300,000 Britons visit the dentist.

• •

THE AVERAGE HOOKER has 22 punters every week. Half of her clients are men with top management or executive jobs.

• •

IN THE 15TH CENTURY, the Pope declared that Halley's Comet was an agent of the devil. He excommunicated it. The Comet's comment was not recorded.

• •

MENTAL ILLNESS results in the loss of 80 million working days a year in England and Wales. This costs employers more than £5 billion a year.

• •

EXPERTS SAY that 93 per cent of everything we worry about never happens.

. . . .

EVERY YEAR 49,000 people need hospital treatment after opening cans, cartons and other food packaging.

. . . .

CASANOVA SUFFERED at least 11 attacks of venereal disease. In one town alone he infected more than 50 people with gonorrhoea.

. . . .

IN PARTS OF SPAIN burial plots are in such short supply that bodies are dug up after six years and compacted so that they take up less space.

here, there and everywhere

VANDALS IN AUSTRIA successfully wrecked a bunker which was designed to withstand an atomic attack.

MORE BIRTHS TAKE PLACE at home in Holland than in any other European country. Is it a coincidence that Holland also has the lowest child mortality rate?

BRIDES IN ANCIENT Cambodia had to give their virginity to the priest – in front of their wedding guests.

THERE ARE 100 species of mammals in France, 99 in Italy and only 44 in Britain.

OPERATING THEATRES in India 4,000 years ago were well lit and ventilated. Surgeons used anaesthetics and antiseptics, and were strictly forbidden to speak during operations in case their breath contaminated the patient's wounds.

. . . .

THE RULERS OF 15th Century Venice insisted that prostitutes sat in their windows with their bare breasts in full view of passers by. The law was passed to divert young men from the 'unnatural aberration' of homosexuality.

. . . .

THE ROMAN CATHOLIC CHURCH in Vincenza, Italy, now accepts confessions by fax. In Israel, you can fax a message to God via Jerusalem's Wailing Wall. In America you can buy a bleeper which will warn you when the Messiah arrives.

. . . .

COMPETITORS IN the Marathon des Sables, a week long running event in the Sahara Desert, shave down the bristles on their toothbrushes to reduce the weight they carry.

• •

IN EGYPT a 25st wife killed her husband by sitting on him.

• •

ONLY SIX OUT of 10 Frenchmen change their underwear daily.

• •

THERE IS A Penis Museum in Tagata, Japan. Visitors can inspect a variety of limp organs floating in preservatives.

• •

TSAR PAUL OF RUSSIA sent soldiers to Siberia for marching out of step.

• •

PROSTITUTES IN Thailand soak their nipples with tranquillisers. Punters who suck the soaked nipples pass out and are then robbed.

• •

THE AUTHORITIES IN Sweden certified Hermann Goering a dangerous drug addict and locked him in an asylum in 1925. During the second World War, Goering became Commander in Chief of the German Luftwaffe.

• •

IN HONG KONG a man arrested for pinching a woman's bottom told magistrates that he did it because he couldn't control his right thumb.

• •

ICELANDERS READ more books than any other group of people.

• •

THE AUTHORITIES IN Tehran have arrested 800 women for wearing sunglasses. Under the Islamic dress code women aren't allowed to wear sunglasses.

• •

THE GABONESE government won't let AIDS sufferers swim in the sea. Shark fishing is an important part of the economy and they are worried that sharks might contract the disease and die.

• •

WOMEN IN SOME African tribes have such long and pendulous breasts that they toss them over their shoulders to keep them out of the way while working.

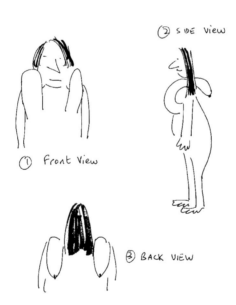

① Front View

② SIDE VIEW

③ BACK VIEW

it's a funny old world

A SIGN PUT UP outside an American library was supposed to say 'You are welcome!' to Filipinos. But the literal translation of the sign was: 'You are circumcised!'

• •

INCONTINENTS and heavy drinkers who pee in lifts shouldn't try it in Singapore. When a new device being tested there detects urine it jams the lift and starts a video camera.

• •

THE CITY OF LOS ANGELES ordered a nightclub to remove a shower cubicle in which nude women danced in front of customers. The city argued that since the shower didn't have suitable access disabled dancers in wheelchairs were prevented from performing.

• •

WHEN AN AFRICAN plane was 300 per cent overbooked, soldiers were called in to deal with the row. They made all the passengers with boarding cards run twice around the aircraft. The fastest qualified for seats on the plane.

• •

JAPANESE MEN who want a prostitute can join a 'One Day Wife Despatch Service'. The women are all housewives who want extra money to help pay the mortgage. (First thought: It is presumably possible that some of the women can't pay the mortgage because their husband is spending all their money on prostitutes. Second thought: How many of the men find themselves hiring their own wives?)

• •

THIS HEADLINE appeared in The New York Times: BUILDING A HUGE ORGAN THE OLD WAY: BY HAND.

• •

A NUDIST COLONY in the South of France has organised patrols to ensure that all visitors remove their clothes. The only item of uniform worn by the patrols is a white cap.

• •

CHINESE TRENDIES are giving their children English names. But they haven't quite got the hang of it. Popular names include: Onion, Civic, Open and Creamy.

• •

A POLICEMAN in the USA was described as 'feloniously flatulent' by his boss and suspended for breaking wind in the faces of two people he arrested. The officer claimed that he suffered from indigestion.

• •

IT IS ILLEGAL TO photograph rabbits in Wyoming between January and April unless you have an official permit.

• •

A DOCTOR REPORTS that a patient who turned up for a cervical smear prepared herself for the encounter by using what she thought was her daughter's 'Feminine Freshness Spray'. However, by accident, she used a disco glitter spray.

• •

A MAN FAINTED while trying to rob a bank with a plastic toy gun.

• •

A SCOTTISH BANK issues transvestites with two cheque guarantee cards – one containing a photograph of them as a man and another with a photograph of them dressed as a woman.

• •

IN 1977 there were 37 Elvis impersonators in the world. In 1993 there were 48,000. Statistically speaking, this means that by the year 2010 one out of every three people will be an Elvis impersonator.

• •

PLUMBERS HAVE BEEN told not to use such sexist terms as 'ball cocks' and 'stop-cocks'. (The politically correct term for a ball cock is a 'float operated valve'.)

• •

A STUDY OF MARRIAGE registers showed that a Mr Cock has married a Miss Prick.

• •

A GANG SPENT the night breaking into a bank in Hampshire – only to discover it had shut four years earlier.

• •

POSTERS HUNG in Tel Aviv to encourage better driving were taken down by the city authorities. The slogan on the posters was: 'Research Proves – Reckless Drivers Have Small Dicks'.

• •

A WOMAN CALLED Lucy Bottom recently married a man called Randy Bonkalot. 'It will be a relief to change my name,' she said. 'I'm fed up with people giggling at me.'

• •

A GUNMAN who held up a petrol station stole sweets worth 50p but then dropped a £10 note of his own.

• •

WHEN POLICE RAIDED a strip club they arrested the club's main attraction – a 66-year-old stripping grandmother. She told them she did it to supplement her pension.

• •

IN THE 14ᵗʰ CENTURY brothel owners frequently complained of unfair competition from convents.

• •

TOURISTS IN AMSTERDAM can visit the Prostitution Information Centre to find out the rates for various sex acts.

• •

A BURGLAR WAS ARRESTED when a woman found him taking a bubble bath in her home.

• •

A MAN WHO WAS arrested while wearing seven pairs of trousers (all with store tags attached to them) told police that he wanted to keep warm.

• •

A GIRL JOCKEY was accused by stewards of influencing a race she won in Australia by wearing brief red knickers. The male jockeys were said to be so mesmerised by her back view that they didn't want to pass her.

• •

IN 1670 A MAN was arrested for trying to smuggle 350 dildos into England.

• •

IN ITALY, police uncovered a ring of prostitutes who were all grandmothers.

• •

AN 83-YEAR OLD man in a wheelchair set out to visit his local library. He got lost and ended up pushing himself along a motorway.

• •

WHEN A GUNMAN tried to rob a bank in Alabama staff told him to queue. By the time he got to the counter, police had arrived.

● ●

WHEN SHE WAS asked why she wanted to change her Christian name a girl called Miss Easy Blow explained that her name caused constant misunderstandings and embarrassment.

For a catalogue of Vernon Coleman's books
please write to:

Publishing House
Trinity Place
Barnstaple
Devon EX32 9HG
England

Telephone   01271 328892
Fax   01271 328768

Outside the UK:
Telephone   +44 1271 328892
Fax   +44 1271 328768

Or visit our website:

www.vernoncoleman.com